ADMINISTRATIVE LAW

First edition. October 7, 2023.

Written by Jagdish Krishanlal Arora.

Table of Contents

Administrative Law

Adapting to New Challenges and Realities

By

Jagdish Krishanlal Arora

Email: techbagg@outlook.com

Chapter 1 - Administrative Law

A dministrative law is a vital component of the legal framework that governs the actions of governments and their various agencies. It deals with the structure, powers, duties, and accountability of these institutions, as well as the rules and procedures they must follow while exercising their authority. This branch of law plays a pivotal role in ensuring that government actions are carried out in a fair, just, and accountable manner. In this comprehensive discussion, we will delve into the multifaceted realm of administrative law, exploring its historical evolution, its contemporary significance, and the challenges it faces in a rapidly changing world.

Historical Roots of Administrative Law

The origins of administrative law can be traced back to ancient civilizations and their practices of governance. In ancient Egypt, for example, there were regulations governing the conduct of government officials and the procedures they followed when interacting with citizens. Similarly, ancient India had a well-developed system of administrative law that encompassed rules for public administration, taxation, and the conduct of officials.

However, it was during the Roman Empire that administrative law began to take shape in a more systematic manner. The Romans had a complex system of administrative procedures and regulations, which laid the groundwork for modern administrative law concepts. The "ius publicum" and the "ius privatum" were two distinct legal systems that governed the actions of government officials and private citizens, respectively.

In medieval Europe, administrative law continued to evolve. The concept of the "rule of law" gained prominence, emphasizing that government officials, including the monarch, were subject to the law and could be held accountable for their actions. This principle laid the foundation for the idea that government powers should be exercised within a legal framework.

The Shift towards Modern Administrative Law

The rapid growth of administrative law in contemporary times can be attributed to various factors, including changes in governance structures, economic developments, and evolving societal needs. The transition from traditional forms of government to modern, democratic states marked a significant turning point in administrative law.

1. The Influence of Individualism and Contractual Freedom: With the rise of individualism and the recognition of private property rights, there was a shift towards limiting the scope of government intervention in the lives of citizens. The concept of contractual freedom gained prominence, emphasizing that individuals should have the freedom to enter into contracts and engage in economic activities without excessive government interference.

2. Minimal Government to Welfare State: In earlier times, governments often seen as primarily responsible for maintaining law and order and defending the country from external threats. Their role was relatively limited. However, as societies grew in complexity and population, the demands on government expanded. The need for better administrative controls to maintain law and order in larger, more diverse societies became apparent.

3. Challenges of Industrialization: The industrial revolution brought about significant changes in society and the economy. It led to the concentration of wealth in the hands of a few, while many workers faced exploitative working conditions, poverty, and child labor. In response, governments began to recognize their role in addressing these social and economic challenges.

4. The Emergence of the Welfare State: The concept of the "social welfare state" gained prominence, emphasizing the government's role as a tool for socio-economic regeneration and the welfare of its citizens. This marked a departure from the earlier notion of a purely "negative" role for government focused on maintaining law and order.

Contemporary Significance of Administrative Law

In the present day, administrative law is a crucial component of modern legal systems around the world. It serves several vital functions:

1. Regulation of Government Powers: Administrative law defines the scope of government authority and the limits within which government agencies can operate. It ensures that government actions are not arbitrary or unchecked.

2. Procedural Fairness: Administrative law lays down rules and procedures that government agencies must follow when making decisions or taking actions that affect individuals or organizations. This includes principles of natural justice, such as the right to a fair hearing and the right to be heard.

3. Accountability and Oversight: Administrative law provides mechanisms for holding government officials and agencies accountable for their actions. This includes judicial review, administrative tribunals, and ombudsman offices that can investigate complaints against government agencies.

4. Protection of Individual Rights: Administrative law safeguards the rights and interests of individuals and groups in their interactions with government authorities. It ensures that individuals are not subjected to unfair treatment or violations of their rights by government agencies.

5. Promotion of Public Interest: Administrative law often aims to balance the interests of individuals with the broader public interest. It ensures that government actions are in line with societal values and goals, such as environmental protection and public health.

Key Elements of Administrative Law

To understand administrative law more comprehensively, it is essential to examine its key elements and principles:

1. Delegation of Powers: Administrative law often involves the delegation of powers by the legislative branch of government to administrative agencies. These agencies are entrusted with specific functions and responsibilities, such as regulating industries, issuing licenses, or enforcing laws.

2. Rulemaking: Administrative agencies have the authority to create rules and regulations that govern various aspects of society. These rules have the force of law and are essential for implementing legislative policies.

3. Adjudication: Administrative agencies can also act as quasi-judicial bodies, making decisions in individual cases. Administrative law sets out the procedures and standards that must be followed in such adjudicatory processes.

4. Judicial Review: One of the critical aspects of administrative law is the concept of judicial review. This allows individuals or organizations to challenge the decisions or actions of administrative agencies in a court of law. Courts can review whether agencies acted within their legal

authority and whether their decisions were reasonable and fair.

5. Due Process: Administrative law incorporates principles of due process, ensuring that individuals are afforded fair treatment when interacting with government agencies. This includes the right to notice, the right to be heard, and the right to an impartial decision-maker.

6. Administrative Discretion: Administrative agencies often have a degree of discretion in making decisions. This discretion is not unlimited and is subject to legal constraints. Administrative law defines the boundaries of this discretion.

7. Oversight Mechanisms: Administrative law provides various oversight mechanisms to check the actions of administrative agencies. These may include administrative tribunals, ombudsman offices, and parliamentary committees.

Challenges and Contemporary Issues in Administrative Law

While administrative law has evolved to address the changing needs of society, it also faces several challenges and contemporary issues in the present day. Some of the notable challenges include:

1. Technological Advancements: The rapid pace of technological advancements has posed challenges for administrative law. Governments and regulatory agencies must adapt to the digital age, addressing issues such as data privacy, cybersecurity, and the regulation of emerging technologies like artificial intelligence.

2. Complexity of Regulations: Over time, regulatory frameworks have become increasingly complex, leading to difficulties in interpretation and compliance. Simplification and consolidation of regulations are needed to make them more accessible and understandable to the public.

3. Globalization: The interconnectedness of economies and societies on a global scale has raised questions about the jurisdiction and authority of administrative agencies. Issues such as international trade, environmental protection, and cross-border disputes require international cooperation and coordination.

4. Accountability and Transparency: Ensuring transparency and accountability in government actions remains a persistent challenge.　　　　　Administrative　　　　　agencies

Chapter 2 - Ancient Administrative Law vs. Modern Administrative Law

―――――

Administrative law, as a concept, has endured through the annals of history, evolving from its rudimentary forms in ancient civilizations to the intricate and multifaceted system it represents in the modern world. A comparative analysis of ancient administrative law and contemporary administrative law highlights the profound transformation this legal discipline has undergone over millennia, reflecting changes in governance, societal needs, and the complexities of modern life.

Ancient Administrative Law: Foundations and Characteristics

1. Limited Government Functions: In ancient times, the scope of government activities was relatively narrow. Governments primarily concerned themselves with matters such as defense against external threats, tax collection, and the maintenance of law and order within their territories. The administrative apparatus was rudimentary, with limited regulatory functions.

2. Voluntary Taxation: Taxation during ancient times was often voluntary and paid on demand. There were no elaborate tax codes or sophisticated revenue collection mechanisms. Taxes were more akin to contributions made by individuals to support the state's basic functions.

3. Maintenance of Peace and Harmony: One of the central functions of ancient administrative law was to maintain peace and harmony within society. Rules and regulations were established to prevent conflicts and ensure a degree of social order.

4. Localized and Decentralized: Administrative systems were typically localized and decentralized. Governance was often fragmented, with various regions or territories governed by local authorities who had a degree of autonomy in decision-making.

5. Simplicity and Limited Regulation: Administrative laws in ancient times were relatively simple and straightforward. They focused on fundamental principles of governance and did not encompass the extensive regulatory frameworks seen in contemporary administrative law.

Modern Administrative Law: Evolution and Complexity

1. Expanded Government Functions: In the modern era, the functions and responsibilities of governments have expanded significantly. Governments are now involved in a wide array of activities, including social welfare, economic regulation, environmental protection, healthcare, education, and more. This expansion reflects the evolving needs of complex societies.

2. Complex and Encompassing Legislation: Modern administrative law is characterized by an extensive body of legislation and regulations. Governments have developed intricate legal frameworks to govern diverse sectors, from financial markets to public health. These laws are often detailed, technical, and subject to continuous updates.

3. Globalization and Interconnectedness: Modern administrative law grapples with the challenges of globalization and interconnectivity. Governments must

navigate complex international relationships, trade agreements, and transnational issues, such as climate change and cybersecurity.

4. Social and Cultural Diversity: Many modern nations are characterized by multi-ethnic and multi-religious societies. This diversity poses challenges in the implementation of administrative law, as different communities may have distinct legal and cultural norms.

5. Balancing Rights and Responsibilities: Contemporary administrative law places a strong emphasis on balancing the rights and responsibilities of individuals, organizations, and the government. Due process, fairness, and accountability mechanisms are integral to this balance.

6. Technological Advancements: The modern era has witnessed rapid technological advancements that have reshaped administrative practices. Issues such as data privacy, digital governance, and the regulation of emerging technologies like artificial intelligence have become prominent concerns.

Challenges and Implications

While modern administrative law has evolved to address the complexities of contemporary governance, it also faces several challenges and implications:

1. Bureaucratic Complexity: The extensive regulations and bureaucracies associated with modern administrative law can be burdensome and lead to inefficiencies. Streamlining and simplifying administrative processes are ongoing challenges.

2. Ensuring Accountability: With the expansion of government functions, ensuring accountability and transparency becomes paramount. Mechanisms for holding

governments and officials accountable must evolve to meet the demands of a modern, interconnected world.

3. Adapting to Cultural Diversity: Managing administrative law in culturally diverse societies requires sensitivity to different legal traditions and norms. Striking a balance between cultural diversity and universal principles of justice is a complex task.

4. Harnessing Technology: The integration of technology into administrative processes presents both opportunities and challenges. Governments must harness technology to enhance efficiency while safeguarding privacy and security.

5. Global Governance: As governments collaborate on global issues, the need for international administrative law and mechanisms for cross-border cooperation become increasingly important.

The evolution of administrative law from its ancient origins to its contemporary complexity is a testament to the ever-changing nature of governance and society. While ancient administrative law focused on basic functions of government and localized regulations, modern administrative law is characterized by its expansive scope, intricate regulations, and global dimensions. It serves as a dynamic framework for governments to address the diverse needs and challenges of the modern world. However, as administrative law continues to adapt to the complexities of contemporary governance, it must also grapple with the need for simplicity, accountability, and responsiveness to the diverse societies it serves.

Chapter 3 - The Comprehensive Scope of Administrative Law

———

Administrative law is a foundational branch of public law that governs the actions and operations of administrative bodies and agencies within a government. It is a multifaceted and dynamic field that addresses a wide range of legal issues and principles related to government authority, accountability, and the protection of individual rights. In this extensive exploration, we delve into the comprehensive scope of administrative law, tracing its historical evolution, examining its fundamental principles, and considering the challenges it faces in a constantly evolving world.

I. Introduction to Administrative Law

Administrative law is the body of law that governs the activities and operations of administrative agencies and bodies within a government. It encompasses the rules, regulations, and legal principles that guide these agencies in their interactions with individuals, organizations, and other government entities. Administrative law plays a pivotal role in ensuring that government actions are carried out fairly, transparently, and within the boundaries of the law. It serves as a critical component of the legal framework in modern democracies, providing a system of checks and balances that helps prevent abuse of power and protects the rights of citizens.

II. Historical Evolution of Administrative Law

To understand the comprehensive scope of administrative law, it is essential to trace its historical evolution. Administrative law has roots in ancient civilizations and has evolved over centuries to meet the changing needs of governance and society.

1. Ancient Administrative Law:

Administrative law, in rudimentary forms, existed in ancient civilizations such as Egypt and India. These early legal systems included rules and procedures governing the conduct of government officials and the administration of justice. While limited in scope, these ancient systems laid the groundwork for more advanced administrative law principles.

2. Roman Influence:

The Roman Empire made significant contributions to administrative law. The Romans developed complex administrative procedures and distinctions between public and private law. Their legal concepts, such as the "ius publicum" and "ius privatum," laid the foundation for modern administrative law's distinction between government actions and private rights.

3. Medieval Europe:

During the Middle Ages in Europe, the concept of the "rule of law" emerged, emphasizing that government officials, including monarchs, were subject to the law. This principle laid the groundwork for the idea that government powers should be exercised within a legal framework, a fundamental tenet of administrative law.

4. Rise of Modern Administrative Law:

The transition from traditional monarchies to modern democracies marked a significant turning point for administrative law. With the advent of democratic governance, administrative law evolved to address the expanded role of governments in society and the need for greater accountability and transparency.

III. Key Principles of Administrative Law

The comprehensive scope of administrative law is defined by several key principles and concepts that govern its application. These principles are fundamental to understanding how administrative law operates and shapes government actions.

1. Delegation of Powers:

Administrative law often involves the delegation of legislative authority from the elected legislature to administrative agencies. These agencies are entrusted with specific functions and responsibilities, such as rulemaking, enforcement, and adjudication.

2. Rulemaking:

Administrative agencies have the authority to create rules and regulations that govern various aspects of society, ranging from environmental protection to financial markets. These rules have the force of law and are essential for implementing legislative policies.

3. Adjudication:

Administrative agencies can act as quasi-judicial bodies, making decisions in individual cases. Administrative law sets out the procedures and standards that must be followed in such adjudicatory processes, including principles of due process.

4. Judicial Review:

One of the central aspects of administrative law is the concept of judicial review. It allows individuals or organizations to challenge the decisions or actions of administrative agencies in a court of law. Courts can review whether agencies acted within their legal authority and whether their decisions were reasonable and fair.

5. Due Process:

Administrative law incorporates principles of due process, ensuring that individuals are afforded fair treatment when interacting with government agencies. This includes the right to notice, the right to be heard, and the right to an impartial decision-maker.

6. Administrative Discretion:

Administrative agencies often have a degree of discretion in making decisions. This discretion is not unlimited and is subject to legal constraints. Administrative law defines the boundaries of this discretion.

7. Oversight Mechanisms:

Administrative law provides various oversight mechanisms to check the actions of administrative agencies. These may include administrative tribunals, ombudsman offices, and parliamentary committees that monitor agency activities.

IV. Administrative Law in Practice

To appreciate the comprehensive scope of administrative law, it is essential to consider how it functions in practice and its real-world applications. Administrative law extends its influence across a wide range of government activities and societal issues.

1. Regulation of Government Actions:

Administrative law regulates all aspects of government actions, including policy development, rulemaking, program implementation, and enforcement. It ensures that government activities are carried out in accordance with established legal principles and procedures.

2. Protection of Individual Rights:

A fundamental purpose of administrative law is to protect the rights and interests of individuals and organizations. It establishes mechanisms for individuals to challenge government decisions that may infringe upon their rights.

3. Economic Regulation:

Administrative agencies often play a central role in regulating economic activities, such as banking, finance, and commerce. They develop rules and regulations to promote fair competition, protect consumers, and ensure market stability.

4. Social Welfare Programs:

Many administrative agencies are responsible for implementing social welfare programs, including healthcare, education, and social services. Administrative law defines the rules and procedures for these programs, ensuring that eligible individuals receive benefits.

5. Environmental Protection:

Environmental agencies are tasked with enforcing regulations aimed at protecting the environment. Administrative law governs the development and enforcement of environmental rules, ensuring compliance with environmental laws.

6. Immigration and Citizenship:

Administrative law plays a crucial role in immigration and citizenship matters. It governs the processes for granting visas, citizenship applications, and deportation proceedings.

7. International Relations:

Administrative law extends to international relations, as governments interact with foreign entities and international organizations. It regulates international agreements, trade agreements, and diplomatic relations.

V. Challenges in Administrative Law

The comprehensive scope of administrative law is not without its challenges and complexities. As governments and societies evolve, administrative law must adapt to new issues and address persistent challenges.

1. Technological Advancements:

The rapid pace of technological advancements presents challenges for administrative law. Issues such as data privacy, cybersecurity, and the regulation of emerging technologies like artificial intelligence require new legal frameworks and regulations.

2. Globalization:

The interconnectedness of economies and societies on a global scale raises questions about the jurisdiction and authority of administrative agencies. Issues such as international trade, environmental protection, and cross-border disputes require international cooperation and coordination.

3. Cultural Diversity:

In multicultural societies, administrative law faces challenges related to cultural diversity. Different communities may have distinct legal and cultural norms, posing complexities in the implementation of administrative law.

4. Balancing Rights and Responsibilities:

Administrative law emphasizes the balance between individual rights and government responsibilities. Striking this balance can be challenging, particularly when it comes to issues such as national security and public safety.

5. Accountability and Transparency:

Ensuring accountability and transparency in government actions remains a persistent challenge. Administrative agencies must be held accountable for their decisions, and mechanisms for oversight and public participation must be strengthened.

6. Evolving Social

and Economic Policies:

As social and economic policies evolve, administrative law must keep pace. Issues such as healthcare reform, climate change mitigation, and income inequality require innovative approaches within the framework of administrative law.

VI. Conclusion: The Enduring Relevance of Administrative Law

In conclusion, administrative law encompasses a vast and comprehensive scope that extends to all facets of modern governance. It is a dynamic field that has evolved over centuries to meet the changing needs of societies and governments. Its principles, including the delegation of powers, due process, and judicial review, provide the framework for accountable and transparent governance.

Administrative law plays a pivotal role in protecting individual rights, regulating government actions, and shaping economic and social policies. It is a critical component of modern democracies, ensuring that governments operate within the bounds of the law and serve the best interests of their citizens.

As administrative law continues to confront challenges related to technology, globalization, cultural diversity, and evolving policies, its enduring relevance remains clear. It is a field that must adapt and innovate to address the complex issues of our time while upholding the principles of justice, fairness, and the rule of law that are at its core. In an ever-changing world, administrative law stands as a safeguard against abuse of power and a protector of the rights and freedoms of individuals and organizations.

The Comprehensive Landscape of Administrative Law: Exploring Types, Functions, and Impact

Administrative law is a multifaceted and intricate field that governs the actions and operations of administrative bodies and agencies within a government. It encompasses a wide array of legal principles, rules, and regulations that guide the functioning of these agencies and their interactions with individuals, organizations, and other government entities. In this comprehensive examination, we delve into the diverse types of administrative laws, their functions, and their profound impact on society, governance, and the legal system.

I. Introduction to Administrative Law

Administrative law constitutes a critical segment of public law that regulates the activities and responsibilities of administrative agencies within a government. These agencies play an essential role in the implementation and enforcement of laws, policies, and regulations across various sectors of society. Administrative law ensures that these agencies act within the bounds of the law, adhere to established procedures, and protect the rights of citizens.

II. Types of Administrative Laws

The realm of administrative law comprises various types of laws and regulations, each serving distinct purposes and addressing specific aspects of government operations and interactions with citizens. The key types of administrative laws include:

1. Statutory Administrative Laws:

Statutory administrative laws are statutes passed by legislative bodies at the national or state level. These laws grant authority to administrative agencies, define their powers and duties, and set out the framework for their operations. Statutes such as the Clean Air Act and the Social Security Act in the United States exemplify statutory administrative laws.

2. Case Law in Administrative Law:

Case law, also known as judicial precedents, plays a pivotal role in administrative law. Courts issue judgments in cases involving disputes between individuals, organizations, and government agencies. These precedents help establish legal principles, interpretations, and precedents that guide administrative decision-making. Case law in administrative law encompasses disputes related to constitutional, civil, and criminal matters, as well as issues like marriage, property succession, and contract disputes.

3. Delegated Legislations:

Delegated legislations refer to rules and regulations promulgated by bodies or authorities other than the national parliament or legislative assembly. These delegated regulations are often granted the force of law and are a fundamental component of administrative law. Administrative agencies frequently issue delegated legislations to provide detailed guidelines and rules for implementing statutory laws. They allow agencies to fill in the details and nuances of laws, ensuring practicality and specificity.

4. Administrative Quasi-Legislations:

Administrative quasi-legislations are akin to laws developed by private entities or societies. These regulations are specific to the jurisdiction where the respective administrative bodies operate and do not have universal applicability. They primarily govern activities within the areas of influence of these bodies and are not binding outside their jurisdiction.

III. Implementation and Function of Administrative Laws

Administrative laws serve a multitude of functions within the governmental framework and the broader legal system:

1. Regulation of Government Actions:

Administrative laws regulate various aspects of government actions, encompassing policy formulation, rulemaking, program execution, and enforcement. These laws ensure that government activities are executed in compliance with established legal principles and procedures.

2. Protection of Individual Rights:

A pivotal role of administrative law is safeguarding the rights and interests of individuals and organizations. It provides mechanisms for individuals to challenge government decisions that may infringe upon their rights, offering redress and protection.

3. Economic Regulation:

Administrative agencies play a central role in economic regulation, overseeing sectors such as banking, finance, and commerce. They create rules and regulations to maintain fair competition, protect consumers, and maintain market stability.

4. Social Welfare Programs:

Administrative agencies are responsible for implementing social welfare programs, including healthcare, education, and social services. Administrative laws define the rules and procedures governing these programs to ensure that eligible individuals receive benefits.

5. Environmental Protection:

Environmental agencies are tasked with enforcing regulations aimed at preserving the environment. Administrative law governs the development and enforcement of environmental rules, ensuring compliance with environmental laws.

6. Immigration and Citizenship:

Administrative law plays a pivotal role in matters related to immigration and citizenship. It regulates processes such as visa issuance, citizenship applications, and deportation proceedings.

7. International Relations:

Administrative law extends to international relations, as governments interact with foreign entities and international organizations. It regulates international agreements, trade relations, and diplomatic interactions.

IV. The Complexities and Challenges of Administrative Law

While administrative law plays a crucial role in governing government actions and protecting individual rights, it is not without complexities and challenges:

1. Technological Advancements:

The rapid progression of technology poses challenges to administrative law. Issues like data privacy, cybersecurity, and the regulation of emerging technologies such as artificial intelligence require new legal frameworks and regulations.

2. Globalization:

The interconnectivity of economies and societies on a global scale raises questions about the jurisdiction and authority of administrative agencies. Matters such as international trade, environmental preservation, and cross-border disputes necessitate international cooperation and coordination.

3. Cultural Diversity:

In multicultural societies, administrative law faces challenges linked to cultural diversity. Different communities may have distinct legal and cultural norms, creating complexities in the implementation of administrative law.

4. Balancing Rights and Responsibilities:

Administrative law places a significant emphasis on the balance between individual rights and government responsibilities. Striking this balance can be challenging, particularly concerning issues like national security and public safety.

5. Accountability and Transparency:

Ensuring accountability and transparency in government actions remains a persistent challenge. Administrative agencies must be held accountable for their decisions, necessitating effective oversight mechanisms and opportunities for public participation.

6. Evolving Social and Economic Policies:

As social and economic policies evolve, administrative law must adapt accordingly. Issues such as healthcare reform, climate change mitigation, and income inequality require innovative approaches within the administrative law framework.

V. The Impact of Administrative Law on Society and Governance

Administrative law exerts a profound influence on society, governance, and the legal system:

1. Protection of Individual Rights:

One of the most significant impacts of administrative law is the protection of individual rights. It ensures that government actions do not infringe upon the fundamental rights and freedoms of citizens, providing mechanisms for redress in case of violations.

2. Rule of Law:

Administrative law upholds the principles of the rule of law, ensuring that governments operate within established legal frameworks and adhere to due process. This fosters trust in government institutions and promotes the fair and equitable treatment of individuals.

3. Accountability and Transparency:

Through mechanisms such as judicial review and public participation, administrative law promotes accountability and transparency in government actions. Citizens have the right to challenge government decisions and hold agencies accountable for their actions.

4. Economic Stability and Fair Competition:

Administrative agencies play a vital role in economic regulation, ensuring fair competition and market stability. This fosters economic growth and protects consumers from unfair business practices.

5. Environmental Conservation:

Administrative law is instrumental in environmental conservation efforts. It enables governments to enforce regulations that protect natural resources and combat environmental degradation.

6. Social Welfare and Equality:

Administrative agencies implement social welfare programs that promote equality and provide essential services to marginalized communities. These programs improve the overall well-being of society.

7. International Relations:

Administrative law governs international relations, shaping agreements and treaties between countries. It facilitates diplomatic interactions and cooperation on global issues.

VI. Conclusion: The Vital Role of Administrative Law

In conclusion, administrative law encompasses a broad and multifaceted spectrum of regulations and principles that govern government actions and interactions with citizens and organizations. It is a dynamic field that continually adapts to the evolving needs of societies and governments. Administrative law, characterized by principles such as due process, judicial review, and transparency, forms the bedrock of modern democracies, ensuring governments operate within the confines of the law and serve the best interests of their constituents.

As administrative law confronts challenges related to technology, globalization, cultural diversity, and evolving policies, its enduring significance remains evident. It is a field that must remain agile and responsive to address the intricate issues of our time while upholding the principles of justice, fairness, and the rule of law that define it. In a world marked by constant change, administrative law stands as a safeguard against the abuse of power and a defender of the rights and freedoms of individuals and organizations. Its impact reverberates throughout society, shaping the way governments operate and individuals experience their rights and   responsibilities.

Chapter 4 - Role of the Judicial System in the Constitution

The judicial system plays a pivotal role in upholding the principles of justice, protecting individual rights, and ensuring that the rule of law prevails within the constitutional framework of any democratic nation. This comprehensive examination explores the indispensable role of the judiciary, its functions, powers, and the significant impact it has on the governance and legal systems of countries worldwide.

I. Introduction: The Essence of Judicial Systems

The judicial system is an integral component of any democratic constitution, serving as the guardian of the rule of law and the protector of individual rights. It functions as a cornerstone of justice, interpreting laws, resolving disputes, and overseeing government actions to ensure they align with the constitution and the law.

II. The Hierarchy of the Judicial System

The structure of the judicial system varies from one country to another, but there are common elements that provide a general understanding of its hierarchy and organization. The key components of this hierarchy typically include:

1. SUPREME COURT:

At the apex of the judicial hierarchy is the Supreme Court, the highest court in the land. The Supreme Court is often the ultimate authority on legal matters, with its decisions serving as precedents for lower courts and guiding the interpretation of laws and the constitution.

2. Appellate Courts:

Beneath the Supreme Court, there are usually intermediate appellate courts. These courts hear appeals from lower courts, review their decisions, and ensure that they are consistent with the law and established legal precedents.

3. Trial Courts:

Trial courts are the entry point for most legal disputes. They are responsible for hearing cases, both civil and criminal, and making initial determinations of guilt or liability. Trials, evidence presentation, and judgments take place at this level.

4. Specialized Courts:

Many countries have specialized courts to handle specific types of cases, such as family courts, juvenile courts, or tax courts. These specialized courts apply specific laws and procedures tailored to their respective areas of jurisdiction.

III. Functions and Powers of the Judiciary

The judiciary carries out a range of crucial functions and exercises specific powers within the constitutional framework:

1. Interpretation of Laws and the Constitution:

A primary function of the judiciary is to interpret laws and the constitution. When legal disputes arise, judges must determine how existing laws and constitutional provisions apply to the case at hand. This interpretation sets legal precedents that guide future cases.

2. Safeguarding Individual Rights:

The judiciary acts as a guardian of individual rights, ensuring that citizens' rights and liberties are protected against unjust violations by any entity, including the government. Courts have the power to issue orders, such as injunctions, to safeguard individual rights.

3. Dispute Resolution:

Courts provide a forum for the resolution of disputes between individuals, organizations, and government entities. They allow parties to present evidence, make arguments, and have an impartial third party render a decision.

4. Judicial Review:

A significant power held by the judiciary is judicial review, which enables courts to examine the constitutionality of laws, regulations, and government actions. If a court finds a law or action unconstitutional, it may declare it void.

5. Checks and Balances:

The judiciary serves as a crucial check on the powers of the other branches of government, including the executive and legislative branches. By reviewing the actions of these branches for constitutionality, the judiciary helps maintain a balance of power.

IV. The Importance of Judicial Independence

Judicial independence is a fundamental principle that ensures the judiciary can carry out its role effectively. It entails judges being free from undue influence or interference from the executive or legislative branches. Judicial independence is vital for upholding the rule of law, protecting individual rights, and maintaining public trust in the judiciary.

V. Precedent and Stare Decisis

Precedent, often referred to as stare decisis, is a fundamental concept in the judicial system. It means that courts are bound by previous decisions, especially those from higher courts. This principle promotes consistency and predictability in the law but also allows for the evolution of legal principles over time.

VI. The Limits of Judicial Power

While the judiciary is essential for upholding the constitution and ensuring justice, it has its limitations:

1. Political Questions:

Courts often refrain from deciding "political questions," which involve matters better suited for the political branches of government. These questions may include foreign policy, military decisions, or certain legislative actions.

2. Enforcement of Judgments:

Courts rely on the executive branch to enforce their judgments. If the executive branch chooses not to enforce a court's decision, it can pose challenges to the effectiveness of the judiciary.

3. Public Opinion:

The authority and legitimacy of the judiciary are partly derived from public trust and acceptance of its decisions. When court decisions run counter to popular opinion, it can strain public trust in the judiciary.

4. Limited Resources:

Courts often face resource constraints, including limited budgets and backlogs of cases. These constraints can affect the timely resolution of cases and access to justice.

VII. The Judiciary's Role in Safeguarding Democracy

A robust and independent judiciary is crucial for the preservation of democracy and the rule of law. It acts as a check on potential abuses of power, ensures accountability, and protects the rights and liberties of citizens. Some key aspects of the judiciary's role in safeguarding democracy include:

1. Separation of Powers:

The judiciary helps maintain the separation of powers by ensuring that the legislative and executive branches do not exceed their constitutional authority.

2. Protecting Minority Rights:

Courts play a vital role in protecting the rights of minority groups, ensuring that they are not marginalized or subject to discrimination by the majority.

3. Preserving the Constitution:

The judiciary is the ultimate guardian of the constitution, ensuring that it is upheld and that all government actions comply with its provisions.

4. Ensuring Fair Elections:

Courts can be called upon to resolve disputes related to elections, including cases of voter suppression, gerrymandering, and election fraud.

VIII. Contemporary Challenges and Issues Facing the Judiciary

The judiciary faces several contemporary challenges and issues that impact its role and functioning:

1. Technological Advancements:

The digital age has introduced new legal questions related to privacy, surveillance, and online communication. Courts must grapple with the implications of rapidly evolving technology.

2. Globalization:

As the world becomes more interconnected, legal issues with international dimensions require judicial consideration. These include cross-border disputes, extradition, and human rights violations in a global context.

3. Cultural and Social Change:

Changing societal norms and attitudes can impact legal interpretations. Issues such as marriage equality, gender rights, and discrimination have brought about shifts in judicial thinking.

4. Access to Justice:

Ensuring equitable access to justice remains a challenge, particularly for marginalized and disadvantaged communities. Courts must address issues of affordability, language barriers, and bias.

IX. Conclusion: The Indispensable Role of the Judiciary

In conclusion, the judiciary plays a pivotal role within the constitutional framework of any nation. It serves as the guardian of the constitution, protector of individual rights, and resolver of disputes. Through its functions of interpretation, judicial review, and checks and balances, the judiciary upholds the rule of law and maintains the delicate balance of power among branches of government.

The significance of judicial independence, the reliance on precedent, and the judiciary's role in safeguarding democracy cannot be overstated. As the world evolves, so too must the judiciary, adapting to new challenges posed by technology, globalization, and social change. Despite these challenges, the judiciary remains a cornerstone of democratic societies, ensuring justice, fairness, and the protection of individual liberties. Its enduring role as the guardian of the constitution underscores its vital importance in upholding the principles of justice and the rule of law.

Chapter 5 - The Objective and Purpose of Administrative Law

———

Administrative law is a foundational component of legal systems in democratic societies. It serves as a framework that regulates the activities of government agencies and their interactions with citizens. This comprehensive exploration delves into the objective and purpose of administrative law, highlighting its critical role in maintaining good governance, protecting individual rights, and ensuring accountability in the public sector.

I. Introduction: The Essence of Administrative Law

Administrative law is a dynamic field of legal practice and scholarship that focuses on the rules, regulations, and principles governing government agencies' actions. It plays a vital role in maintaining the rule of law, upholding the principles of justice, and safeguarding citizens' rights in their interactions with the government. Administrative law is a multifaceted discipline that addresses various objectives and purposes.

II. The Evolution of Administrative Law

Administrative law has evolved significantly over time, adapting to the changing needs and complexities of modern governance. Its development can be traced through historical milestones, including the rise of administrative agencies, the expansion of the regulatory state, and the increasing need for legal mechanisms to address administrative decisions and actions.

III. Key Objectives of Administrative Law

Administrative law serves several key objectives, each of which contributes to its overarching purpose:

1. Rule of Law:

At its core, administrative law seeks to ensure that government actions are conducted within the bounds of the law. It upholds the principle that no one, including government officials and agencies, is above the law.

2. Protecting Individual Rights:

One of the primary objectives of administrative law is to protect the rights and interests of individuals when they interact with government entities. This includes safeguarding civil liberties, property rights, and due process.

3. Promoting Accountability:

Administrative law establishes mechanisms for holding government agencies and officials accountable for their actions. This includes processes for reviewing and challenging administrative decisions.

4. Ensuring Fairness and Justice:

Administrative law strives to ensure that administrative procedures are fair, just, and transparent. It provides a framework for citizens to seek redress when they believe they have been treated unfairly.

5. Regulatory Oversight:

Administrative law facilitates the oversight of government regulations and policies, ensuring that they are necessary, proportionate, and consistent with legislative intent.

6. Efficient Government Operations:

Efficiency is another objective of administrative law. It aims to streamline government processes, reduce bureaucratic obstacles, and improve the delivery of public services.

IV. The Purpose of Administrative Law

Administrative law serves a broad and interconnected set of purposes that collectively contribute to the effective functioning of government and the protection of citizens' rights:

1. Balancing Government Power:

Administrative law acts as a check on the exercise of government authority, preventing the abuse of power and ensuring that agencies act within their delegated authority.

2. Resolving Disputes:

It provides mechanisms for resolving disputes between individuals and government agencies. Administrative tribunals and courts play a crucial role in this regard.

3. Promoting Transparency:

Administrative law promotes transparency by requiring government agencies to disclose information, hold public hearings, and provide reasons for their decisions.

4. Facilitating Administrative Processes:

It establishes procedures and rules that guide the day-to-day operations of government agencies, ensuring that they function effectively and efficiently.

5. Adjudicating Administrative Matters:

Administrative law empowers administrative tribunals and courts to adjudicate matters related to administrative decisions, ensuring that justice is served.

6. Safeguarding the Public Interest:

Administrative law aims to protect the public interest by ensuring that government actions and regulations align with societal values and priorities.

V. The Role of Administrative Law in Modern Governance

In modern governance, administrative law plays a central role in maintaining the delicate balance between government authority and individual rights. It addresses contemporary challenges, including the regulation of emerging technologies, environmental protection, and the need for efficient public administration.

VI. Challenges and Criticisms of Administrative Law

Despite its crucial role, administrative law faces various challenges and criticisms, including concerns about excessive bureaucracy, delays in administrative processes, and issues related to judicial deference to administrative agencies. These challenges underscore the need for ongoing reform and improvement in administrative law systems.

VII. Conclusion: The Enduring Importance of Administrative Law

In conclusion, administrative law serves as a cornerstone of modern governance, addressing a multitude of objectives and purposes. It is essential for upholding the rule of law, protecting individual rights, promoting accountability, and ensuring fairness in government actions. As societies continue to evolve, administrative law remains adaptable and vital, providing a legal framework that empowers citizens and holds governments accountable to the principles of justice and good governance.

Chapter 6 - Implementation of Administrative Law

‗‗‗‗

Administrative law is the cornerstone of effective governance in modern democracies. It serves as the guiding framework for the operation of government at various levels, from the national to the local. This comprehensive exploration delves into the intricacies of implementing administrative law, shedding light on the multifaceted nature of this vital legal domain.

I. Introduction: The Significance of Administrative Law Implementation

The implementation of administrative law is a complex and essential aspect of government functioning. It is the means by which the rules, regulations, and principles outlined in administrative law are put into practice. This process ensures that government agencies operate within the boundaries set by law and that citizens' rights are protected in their interactions with the government.

II. The Expanding Scope of Administrative Law Implementation

The scope of administrative law implementation has expanded significantly over time. As governments have grown in size and complexity, so too have the challenges associated with effectively implementing administrative law. This section explores the historical context of administrative law implementation and its evolution to meet the demands of modern governance.

III. Key Components of Administrative Law Implementation

Implementing administrative law involves a series of interconnected components, each playing a crucial role in ensuring the proper functioning of government. These components include:

1. Administrative Procedures:

Administrative law outlines specific procedures that government agencies must follow when making decisions, issuing regulations, and interacting with the public. These procedures promote transparency, fairness, and accountability.

2. Regulatory Compliance:

Government agencies are responsible for ensuring that their actions and regulations comply with administrative law. This involves reviewing existing regulations, making necessary changes, and seeking legal guidance to avoid legal challenges.

3. Judicial Oversight:

The judiciary plays a pivotal role in administrative law implementation. Courts are responsible for interpreting administrative law, reviewing government actions, and adjudicating disputes between citizens and government agencies. Judicial decisions set legal precedents that guide future administrative actions.

4. Enforcement Mechanisms:

Administrative law provides mechanisms for enforcing government decisions and regulations. This includes the use of administrative tribunals, sanctions, fines, and other enforcement tools to ensure compliance.

5. Citizen Engagement:

Citizens have the right to engage with government agencies, challenge administrative decisions, and seek redress for perceived injustices. Administrative law guarantees citizens a voice in the governance process.

IV. The Role of Administrative Agencies in Implementation

Government agencies are at the forefront of administrative law implementation. They are responsible for executing policies, enforcing regulations, and interacting with citizens. These agencies must navigate a complex web of legal requirements and procedures to ensure that their actions align with administrative law.

V. Challenges in Administrative Law Implementation

While administrative law is essential for effective governance, it is not without its challenges. Some of the key challenges include:

1. Bureaucratic Hurdles:

Government bureaucracies can be cumbersome, leading to delays and inefficiencies in administrative law implementation. Streamlining administrative processes is an ongoing challenge.

2. Interpretation and Ambiguity:

Administrative law can be complex and open to interpretation. This can lead to disputes and legal challenges over the meaning and application of specific regulations.

3. Resource Constraints:

Limited resources, both human and financial, can hinder effective administrative law implementation. Government agencies must balance competing priorities and allocate resources judiciously.

4. Evolving Regulations:

As society evolves, so do the regulations needed to address new challenges. Government agencies must adapt and update regulations to remain relevant and effective.

5. Public Perception:

Public perception of administrative law and government agencies can influence compliance and cooperation. Building trust and confidence in administrative processes is an ongoing endeavor.

VI. Administrative Law Implementation in Practice

To illustrate the practical aspects of administrative law implementation, this section provides real-world examples and case studies. These examples showcase how administrative law is applied in various contexts, from environmental regulation to immigration policy.

VII. Conclusion: The Imperative of Effective Administrative Law Implementation

In conclusion, the implementation of administrative law is a multifaceted process that underpins the functioning of government in democratic societies. It ensures that government actions are conducted in accordance with the law, protects citizens' rights, and upholds the principles of justice and accountability. While challenges persist, the ongoing commitment to effective administrative law implementation is essential for the continued success of modern governance. As governments evolve and face new challenges, the principles and practices of administrative law will remain a vital guide for navigating the complexities of governance.

Chapter 7 - The Role of Administrative Officers

———

Administrative officers are the unsung heroes of government, responsible for executing policies, enforcing regulations, and ensuring the smooth functioning of public administration. This comprehensive exploration delves into the multifaceted role of administrative officers, addressing their powers, limitations, and the critical role they play in upholding the principles of administrative law.

I. Introduction: Understanding Administrative Officers

Administrative officers are government officials tasked with carrying out the day-to-day functions of public administration. They serve as a bridge between government policies and the citizens they impact. This section provides an overview of the significance of administrative officers in the governance structure.

II. Who Are Administrative Officers?

Administrative officers come from various backgrounds and hold diverse positions within government agencies. They can include civil servants, law enforcement officers, regulatory officials, and more. Their roles may vary widely depending on the level of government—national, state, or local—and the specific agency they work for.

III. The Nature and Powers Exercised by Administrative Officers

Administrative officers wield significant powers in the execution of government functions. These powers can include:

1. Regulatory Authority:

Administrative officers often have the authority to create, implement, and enforce regulations within their areas of jurisdiction. This authority is essential for maintaining order and ensuring compliance with government policies.

2. Decision-Making:

Administrative officers make decisions that impact individuals, organizations, and communities. They may adjudicate disputes, issue permits, grant licenses, and more, all while adhering to established laws and regulations.

3. Law Enforcement:

In the realm of law enforcement, administrative officers play a critical role in maintaining public safety and order. They have the power to enforce laws, conduct investigations, and take actions to protect citizens.

4. Administrative Discretion:

Administrative officers often have a degree of discretion in their decision-making. This discretion allows them to adapt to unique circumstances while still operating within the bounds of the law.

IV. Limitations and Restrictions on Administrative Powers

While administrative officers hold significant powers, these powers are not unlimited. Administrative law imposes restrictions and limitations to prevent abuse and ensure fairness. Some key limitations include:

1. Legal Framework:

Administrative officers must operate within the framework of established laws, regulations, and policies. They cannot create rules or policies that are in conflict with existing legal norms.

2. Due Process:

Individuals affected by administrative decisions have the right to due process. This includes the right to be heard, the right to appeal decisions, and protection against arbitrary actions.

3. Accountability:

Administrative officers are accountable for their actions. They must justify their decisions and actions, and they can be subject to legal scrutiny and oversight.

4. Transparency:

Transparency is crucial in administrative decision-making. Administrative officers are often required to provide reasons for their decisions and make information available to the public.

V. Preventing the Misuse of Administrative Powers

Preventing the misuse of administrative powers is a paramount concern. This section explores strategies and mechanisms for ensuring that administrative officers do not abuse their authority. Some of these strategies include:

1. Training and Education:

Proper training and education for administrative officers can help them understand the boundaries of their powers and the importance of adhering to legal norms.

2. Internal Oversight:

Government agencies often have internal oversight mechanisms to review and evaluate the actions of administrative officers. This oversight helps identify and address any misconduct or misuse of powers.

3. Legal Remedies:

Citizens adversely affected by the misuse of administrative powers have legal remedies available to them. They can seek redress through administrative appeals, ombudsman offices, or the judicial system.

VI. Implementation and Regulation by Administrative Authorities

The effective implementation and regulation of administrative powers are essential for maintaining the rule of law and ensuring that government functions smoothly. Administrative authorities play a central role in this process, and this section explores their responsibilities and challenges.

VII. Remedies for Those Affected by Misuse of Powers

When administrative officers misuse their powers and harm individuals or organizations, there are remedies available to those adversely affected. These remedies can include:

1. Administrative Appeals:

Individuals can often appeal administrative decisions within the government agency itself. This provides an avenue for reviewing and potentially overturning unfair or unlawful decisions.

2. Ombudsman Offices:

Many governments have ombudsman offices that investigate complaints against government agencies and officials. These offices can recommend corrective actions and promote accountability.

3. Judicial Review:

Citizens can seek redress through the judicial system if they believe their rights have been violated by administrative actions. Courts can review administrative decisions and issue rulings based on the principles of administrative law.

VIII. The Evolution of Administrative Law and the Role of Administrative Officers

Administrative law has evolved significantly over time to address the complexities of modern governance. It has become a dynamic field that balances the need for efficient administration with the protection of individual rights. Administrative officers are central to this evolution, as they are tasked with upholding the principles of administrative law in their daily work.

IX. Conclusion: The Guardians of Administrative Law

In conclusion, administrative officers are entrusted with substantial powers and responsibilities in the execution of government functions. While these powers are essential for effective governance, they must be exercised within the bounds of administrative law to prevent abuse and protect the rights of citizens. The role of administrative officers is multifaceted, requiring a deep understanding of legal norms and a commitment to upholding the principles of justice, fairness, and accountability. As guardians of administrative law, these officers play a critical role in ensuring that government actions serve the best interests of society while respecting individual rights and the rule of law.

Chapter 8 - The Significance and Evolution of Administrative Law

———

I. The Growing Relevance of Administrative Law

The escalating importance of administrative law in contemporary governance.

The need for public awareness and understanding of administrative rules.

II. Administrative Law: A Multifaceted Phenomenon

Examining administrative law as a global phenomenon.

Comparative analysis of administrative law vis-à-vis other legal domains.

The role of administrative law in maintaining checks and balances.

III. The Rise of Administrative Law Education

The emergence of administrative law as a specialized field of study.

The parallels between administrative law and criminal law.

The role of educational institutions in producing competent administrative law practitioners.

IV. The Judiciary's Role in Administrative Oversight

The judiciary's critical role in monitoring and enforcing administrative laws.

Challenges posed by the increasing complexity of administrative regulations.

The need for judicial coordination and interpretation of administrative laws.

V. Addressing Misuse of Administrative Laws

Instances of political leaders and authorities misusing administrative laws for personal or political gain.

The consequences of such misuse on communities, individuals, and opposition parties.

The call for a more impartial and knowledgeable approach to crafting administrative laws.

VI. Crafting Administrative Laws: A Call for Expertise

The necessity of administrative laws being formulated by individuals with legal knowledge and experience.

Advocating for a collaborative approach involving legal experts and non-criminal public representatives.

The impact of well-crafted administrative laws on ensuring justice and fairness in governance.

VII. The Ongoing Development of Administrative Law

A review of the current state of administrative law as an evolving legal discipline.

Examining the balance between the expansion of administrative regulations and the protection of individual rights.

Identifying the gaps in administrative law and the challenges in safeguarding people's rights.

VIII. Administrative Law in Action: Challenges and Spectacles

The practical application of administrative law in addressing arbitrary exercises of power.

Instances of public inaction and media scrutiny in the face of administrative law abuses.

The role of the judiciary in intervening and upholding the rule of law.

IX. Administrative Law as the Guardian of Governance

Recapitulation of the increasing relevance and importance of administrative law.

The essential role of administrative law in ensuring accountability, justice, and fairness in governance.

The ongoing need for the development and refinement of administrative laws to meet the evolving challenges of contemporary society.

Chapter 9 - The Balance of Power: Ensuring Accountability and Justice

I. The Watchdog Role of the Judiciary

The judiciary as a guardian against arbitrary administrative actions.

The necessity of a balance between administrative authority and judicial redressal.

The challenges faced by citizens in seeking justice and the need for accessible redressal mechanisms.

II. Addressing Grievances Beyond Costly Court Cases

The inequity in access to justice and the financial burden of court cases.

The call for alternative redressal mechanisms for citizens unable to afford legal proceedings.

The potential benefits of reduced caseloads and improved efficiency for both the government and the judiciary.

III. Administrative Laws: Regulating Lives and Liberties

The pervasive influence of administrative laws on citizens' daily lives.

Balancing individual freedoms with societal needs in administrative regulations.

The misconception of administrative law solely serving the interests of authorities.

IV. Striking a Balance Between Power and Justice

Recognizing the inherent conflict between power and justice in society.

Administrative law's mission to prevent abuse of governmental power.

The role of administrative laws in promoting social welfare and addressing complex socio-economic issues.

V. Safeguarding Rights Through Administrative Laws

The misunderstood purpose of administrative law as a tool against citizens.

The importance of administrative laws in protecting the rights of both government officers and citizens.

The judiciary's vital role in ensuring accountability and justice.

VI. The Judiciary's Role in Accountability

The importance of quick and cost-effective justice.

Promoting public interest litigations to serve the common good.

Providing bail for trials when necessary to uphold the principle of justice.

Taking into account the vulnerability of marginalized groups, including the elderly and the impoverished.

VII. Holding Authorities Accountable

The need for accountability in administrative law enforcement.

Ensuring authorities are held responsible for implementing social and economic policies.

The judiciary's role as an impartial arbitrator between the administration and citizens.

VIII. The Impact of Delayed Justice

The consequences of delayed decisions on the number of pending court cases.

The importance of timely resolutions for efficiency in the judicial system.

Striving for prompt decisions to reduce the backlog of cases.

IX. Expanding Accountability to the Public

The evolving role of administrative officers' accountability.

The growing significance of public interest litigations in holding authorities accountable.

Cases of information concealment and favoritism in land allotments and schemes.

Ensuring transparency and fairness in the allocation of public resources.

X. Upholding Justice Through Administrative Law

The importance of maintaining a balance of power between administration and the judiciary.

The role of administrative law in promoting accountability and justice.

The ongoing need for accessible redressal mechanisms and the protection of citizen rights in the evolving landscape of governance.

I. The Watchdog Role of the Judiciary

The judiciary plays a pivotal role in the governance of a nation by acting as a vigilant watchdog over the actions of the administration. It serves as a check against arbitrary exercise of power by administrative authorities, ensuring that the rights and liberties of citizens are safeguarded. However, to maintain a just and equitable society, it is imperative to strike a delicate balance between the authority wielded by the administration and the avenues for judicial redressal available to citizens.

In this regard, it becomes evident that a harmonious equilibrium must be established between the power vested in administrative bodies and the mechanisms for seeking justice. While the judiciary stands as the guardian of the law, it is essential to address the challenges that ordinary citizens face in accessing justice and establish alternative pathways for resolving grievances. This not only serves the interests of justice but also contributes to the efficient functioning of both the government and the judiciary.

II. Addressing Grievances Beyond Costly Court Cases

One of the primary concerns in the current legal landscape is the lack of equitable access to justice. Legal proceedings often come with substantial financial burdens, preventing many citizens from seeking redress through the courts. The prohibitive costs associated with litigation disproportionately affect the vulnerable and marginalized sections of society. To bridge this gap, there is an urgent need to explore alternative avenues for addressing grievances.

Introducing accessible redressal mechanisms that do not place a heavy financial burden on citizens can significantly improve the overall efficiency of the justice system. By reducing the number of cases that reach the courts, these mechanisms can expedite the resolution of genuine disputes, benefiting both the government and the judiciary in terms of resource allocation and time management.

III. Administrative Laws: Regulating Lives and Liberties

Administrative laws, by their very nature, play an integral role in governing citizens' lives and liberties. They prescribe the rules and regulations that dictate the parameters within which individuals can exercise their rights and freedoms. These laws extend into various facets of daily life, from land use and business operations to environmental protection and public services.

However, there exists a common misconception that administrative laws primarily serve the interests of the authorities. In reality, these laws are designed to strike a delicate balance between individual freedoms and the collective needs of society. They are not tools to restrict citizens' rights but mechanisms to ensure that these rights are exercised within a framework that promotes the greater good.

IV. Striking a Balance Between Power and Justice

Society is inherently marked by the tension between power and justice. Administrative law emerges as a response to this tension, seeking to prevent the abuse of power while promoting the principles of justice and equity. It embodies the collective will to establish a system that not only addresses individual grievances but also tackles complex socio-economic issues.

The mission of administrative law is not to wield power arbitrarily but to ensure that governmental actions are rooted in legality and fairness. It serves as a safeguard against authoritarianism and strives to uphold the principles of good governance. Administrative laws, therefore, function as vital instruments for advancing social welfare and addressing the multifaceted challenges of contemporary society.

V. Safeguarding Rights Through Administrative Laws

One of the common misinterpretations of administrative law is that it is designed to curtail citizens' rights. In reality, administrative laws serve as the guardians of rights, protecting both government officers and citizens. These laws establish a framework within which administrative actions are conducted, ensuring that they adhere to legal and constitutional standards.

The judiciary assumes a pivotal role in upholding the principles of administrative law. It acts as an impartial adjudicator, ensuring that government authorities are held accountable for their actions. This oversight is not aimed at stifling administrative processes but at guaranteeing their adherence to the rule of law. Through the judiciary's involvement, citizens are provided with a mechanism to seek justice and hold administrative bodies accountable.

VI. The Judiciary's Role in Accountability

Efficiency in the judicial system is paramount to ensuring justice for all citizens. To this end, it is crucial to promote quick and cost-effective justice. Public interest litigations, which serve the common good, must be encouraged to prevent the abuse of power and protect citizens' rights. Moreover, bail for trials should be readily available when necessary to uphold the principle of justice.

The vulnerability of marginalized groups, including the elderly and the impoverished, should be taken into account when deciding cases that lack merit. Such cases often burden both the courts and those who have little means to navigate complex legal processes.

VII. Holding Authorities Accountable

Accountability is a cornerstone of administrative law. Authorities must be held responsible for implementing social and economic policies effectively. The judiciary serves as an impartial arbitrator, ensuring that the actions of administrative bodies are in line with legal and constitutional principles. This accountability is not a tool against administrative authorities but a means to protect the rights of citizens and maintain the integrity of the administrative process.

VIII. The Impact of Delayed Justice

Delayed decisions have a profound impact on the number of pending court cases, straining the judicial system. Timely resolutions are essential for the efficient functioning of the judiciary. Reducing the backlog of cases necessitates prompt decisions, which can be achieved by streamlining processes and optimizing resource allocation.

IX. Expanding Accountability to the Public

The evolving landscape of administrative law calls for an expansion of accountability beyond the judiciary. Administrative officers are increasingly being held accountable to the public, particularly in cases involving information concealment and favoritism in resource allocation. Transparency and fairness in the distribution of public resources are critical to upholding the principles of justice and equity.

X. Upholding Justice Through Administrative Law

The balance of power between administration and the judiciary is vital for the well-being of any society. Administrative law, far from being a tool against citizens, is a mechanism that promotes accountability, justice, and good governance. As governance becomes more complex, the need for accessible redressal mechanisms and the protection of citizen rights remains paramount. Administrative law serves as a safeguard against the abuse of power and ensures that the principles of justice and equity prevail in the governance of nations.

Chapter 10 - Delegation of Powers to Multiple Institutions

I. The Imperative of Separation of Powers

The concept of the separation of powers as fundamental to administrative laws.

Ensuring impartiality by dividing the powers of legislation, administration, and adjudication.

The historical and philosophical underpinnings of the separation of powers.

II. Application Across All Types of Laws

Extending the principle of separation of powers to various legal domains.

The incompatibility of legislating and implementing laws within the same body.

The role of courts as arbiters of disputes and impartial decision-makers.

III. The Role of the Courts in Ensuring Justice

The judiciary's function as a forum for determining the rightness or wrongness of actions.

The practical implementation of court orders by law enforcement agencies.

The consequences of legislative and executive bodies overseeing their laws' execution.

IV. Avoiding Monopoly and Concentration of Power

The dangers of concentrating power within a single individual or institution.

The imperfections inherent in any person or entity, necessitating checks and balances.

The distribution of powers across multiple institutions for comprehensive oversight.

V. Safeguarding Against Arbitrary Decision-Making

The need for impartiality in decision-making processes.

An example from police stations illustrating the consequences of combining lawmaking and law enforcement.

The prevalence of bribery and fear-driven decisions when powers are concentrated.

VI. Constitutional Frameworks and Checks on Power

The inclusion of separation of powers in major constitutions worldwide.

Distribution of powers between the judiciary, administration, and political leadership.

Legislative checks and balances to prevent the unilateral passage of laws.

VII. The Judiciary's Role as an Impartial Arbiter

The unique role of the judiciary in adjudicating disputes.

The distinction between executive and legislative authorities.

Scrutiny of decisions by higher courts to ensure justice and legality.

VIII. Accountability in Legislative and Executive Branches

The accountability of the executive to the legislative body.

The role of the President, Prime Minister, and Cabinet in implementing administrative decisions.

The necessity for collective responsibility in government decision-making.

IX. Judicial Independence and Decision-Making

The significance of judicial independence in ensuring impartiality.

The process of appointing judges and their accountability.

The judiciary's role in upholding the principles of justice and equity.

X. The Power of the People and the Constitution

Empowering citizens in the decision-making process.

The distribution of power from the public to the highest levels of government.

Chapter 11 - The constitution's recognition of the principle of separation of powers and its impact on fundamental rights and natural justice.

I. The Imperative of Separation of Powers

The concept of the separation of powers is fundamental to the effective implementation of administrative laws. It recognizes that the entity responsible for enacting laws cannot simultaneously execute them or adjudicate disputes related to their application. This principle applies universally across different types of laws, whether they are judicial, administrative, criminal, or penal codes. The separation of powers is not a modern invention but a concept that has existed for centuries, championed by various philosophers throughout history. It ensures impartiality in the governance process and prevents abuses of authority.

II. Application Across All Types of Laws

The separation of powers is not limited to administrative laws; it extends to all legal domains. It acknowledges the inherent conflict of interest when the same body that creates laws is responsible for their execution. For instance, in the realm of criminal law, the judiciary serves as the arbiter of disputes, determining the guilt or innocence of individuals, while law enforcement agencies, such as the police, implement the court's orders. Combining these functions within a single entity can undermine the pursuit of justice.

III. The Role of the Courts in Ensuring Justice

The judiciary plays a pivotal role in upholding the principles of administrative law. It acts as a forum where disputes are resolved, and the rightness or wrongness of actions is determined. However, the practical implementation of court orders falls under the purview of law enforcement agencies. When legislative and executive bodies oversee their laws' execution, it can lead to conflicts of interest and compromises in impartiality.

IV. Avoiding Monopoly and Concentration of Power

The concentration of power in one individual or institution poses a significant risk to society. No person or entity is infallible, and the potential for abuse of authority exists when unchecked power is wielded. The principle of separation of powers seeks to distribute authority among multiple institutions, thereby establishing checks and balances to prevent abuses and safeguard individual rights.

V. Safeguarding Against Arbitrary Decision-Making

Impartiality in decision-making processes is essential for maintaining the rule of law. For example, consider police stations where decisions are made independently of the courts due to fear or the high costs associated with litigation. This can lead to corruption and unjust decisions made under duress. Separating the powers of lawmaking and law enforcement helps mitigate these risks.

VI. Constitutional Frameworks and Checks on Power

The separation of powers is a foundational concept enshrined in the constitutions of many countries worldwide. It entails the distribution of powers among the judiciary, the administration, and the political leadership. It also includes legislative checks and balances to prevent the unilateral passage of laws. This framework ensures that no single entity can dominate the decision-making process.

VII. The Judiciary's Role as an Impartial Arbiter

The judiciary assumes a unique role in society as the impartial arbiter of disputes. It stands apart from executive and legislative authorities, serving as a guardian of justice and legality. Decisions made by lower courts are subject to scrutiny by higher courts, ensuring that justice is not compromised and that the rule of law prevails.

VIII. Accountability in Legislative and Executive Branches

Accountability is a cornerstone of democratic governance. The executive branch is accountable to the legislative body, which oversees and scrutinizes its actions. This includes the President, Prime Minister, and Cabinet, who implement administrative decisions. Collective responsibility within the government ensures that decisions are made collectively and that the trust of the legislative body is not lost.

IX. Judicial Independence and Decision-Making

Judicial independence is vital to upholding the principles of justice and equity. Judges are appointed through a process that prioritizes impartiality, and they are held accountable for their decisions. The judiciary plays a crucial role in ensuring that justice is served, even when it involves holding powerful individuals or entities accountable for their actions.

X. The Power of the People and the Constitution

Ultimately, the power of governance rests with the people. The distribution of power, from the public to the highest levels of government, is integral to the principles of democracy and justice. The constitution recognizes the importance of the separation of powers, which impacts fundamental rights, natural justice, and the overall governance of a nation.

In summary, the principle of separation of powers is essential to the effective implementation of administrative laws and the preservation of justice. It prevents the concentration of power, upholds impartiality, and ensures that no single entity can dominate the decision-making process. As societies continue to evolve, the principles of separation of powers remain a critical safeguard against abuses of authority and violations of individual rights.

Chapter 12 - The Rule of Law Concept and Its Basic Principles

———

I. The Primacy of the Rule of Law

The rule of law as a fundamental principle in almost all constitutional frameworks.

Historical roots tracing back to ancient times and the supremacy of law over arbitrary rule.

The transformation of law from "God's Law" to modern legal systems.

II. Understanding the Essence of the Rule of Law

Dissecting the meaning of "The Rule of Law."

The rule of law as a doctrine of political morality.

Balancing individual rights and state power, freedom and justice, equality and responsibility.

III. The Historical Evolution of the Rule of Law

Tracing the origins of the rule of law to Roman times.

The concept of "God's Law" and its eventual transition to modern legal systems.

The moral and cultural dimensions of the rule of law.

IV. Core Principles of the Rule of Law

The doctrine's foundation in the supremacy of law.

The role of the rule of law in maintaining discipline and order in society.

Natural law, historical ideals, and the influence of philosophers in shaping its principles.

V. Ensuring Supremacy of Rights

The principle of the supremacy of rights.

Equality before the law as a fundamental aspect of the rule of law.

The prevalence of the legal spirit and the limitation of authority to prevent misuse.

VI. Administrative Officers and Their Role

The distinction between administrative officers and legal authorities.

The monitoring of administrative actions by the courts of law.

The requirement that justice be implemented through known legal principles and not through arbitrary actions.

VII. Eliminating Arbitrary Power and Privilege

The rule of law's elimination of arbitrariness and privilege.

The authority of the government and its political leaders being subject to the same laws as other citizens.

The prevention of arbitrary arrests, punishments, and torture.

VIII. Legal Recourse and Due Process

The central role of the legal system in upholding the rule of law.

Opposition to arbitrary and autocratic governments.

The necessity of legal proceedings for arrests, punishments, or violations of administrative law.

IX. Checks on Government Powers

The importance of limiting government's discretionary powers.

The significance of court intervention in cases where power is exercised arbitrarily.

Safeguarding freedom by preventing excessive government interference.

X. Contemporary Challenges to the Rule of Law

Addressing complexities in modern governments.

Combating detention by law enforcement authorities with arbitrary powers.

Ensuring equal access to justice for all citizens.

I. Introduction: The Primacy of the Rule of Law

The rule of law stands as a cornerstone principle in the constitutions of nearly all countries. It transcends time, culture, and ideology, echoing the ancient belief that law, not arbitrary authority, should govern society. While history reveals its roots dating back to Roman times, the concept of law was once equated with "God's Law." Over the centuries, this evolved into modern legal systems. "The Rule of Law" transcends mere governance; it epitomizes the "political morality of the state." It seeks the equilibrium between individual rights and state power, freedom and justice, equality and responsibility. In essence, it embodies the essence of a free and civil society and harmonizes law with moral virtue.

II. Understanding the Essence of the Rule of Law

"The Rule of Law" is neither a mere "rule" nor "law." It constitutes a doctrine, a moral imperative that centers on the ascendancy of law over arbitrary dominion. At its core, it strives for a harmonious equilibrium between "rights" and "power," nurturing a society where justice prevails. It intertwines legality with morality, breathing life into the concept of "political morality of the state."

III. The Historical Evolution of the Rule of Law

The historical evolution of the rule of law can be traced back to Roman jurisprudence, where law began to overshadow the whims of rulers. The notion of "God's Law" held sway for centuries before yielding to modern legal systems. These transformations are not just legal but deeply cultural and moral, reflecting the collective moral conscience of societies.

IV. Core Principles of the Rule of Law

At its heart, the rule of law is underpinned by the doctrine of the supremacy of law. It represents a fundamental need for order and discipline in society. The roots of this concept lie in natural law, historical ideals, and the profound influence of philosophers who molded its foundational principles of justice and equality.

V. Ensuring Supremacy of Rights

The rule of law champions the supremacy of rights, ensuring that no one, regardless of their station, is above the law. Equality before the law is a bedrock principle, and the legal spirit pervades every facet of society, acting as a check on authority to prevent its abuse.

VI. Administrative Officers and Their Role

Central to the rule of law is the distinction between administrative officers and legal authorities. Administrative actions are subject to rigorous scrutiny by the courts of law. Justice is to be dispensed through established legal principles and not through the arbitrary actions of officials. Authority does not signify a lack of rules; instead, it operates within the confines of legality.

VII. Eliminating Arbitrary Power and Privilege

The rule of law dismantles the pillars of arbitrariness and privilege. The government's authority, including that of its political leaders, is tethered to the same laws governing all citizens. It prohibits arbitrary arrests, punishments, and torture, upholding the sanctity of due process.

VIII. Legal Recourse and Due Process

Legal recourse through recognized courts is central to the rule of law. It stands in stark opposition to arbitrary and autocratic regimes, affirming that government actions require legal proceedings. Arrests, punishments, or violations of administrative law should not occur without due process.

IX. Checks on Government Powers

Crucial to the rule of law is the containment of government's discretionary powers. Courts play a pivotal role in cases where power is wielded arbitrarily, ensuring that government interference does not infringe on citizens' freedoms.

X. Contemporary Challenges to the Rule of Law

Modern governments are marked by complexity, presenting fresh challenges. Arbitrary detention by law enforcement authorities, armed with sweeping powers, poses a risk to the rule of law. Ensuring equal access to justice for all, regardless of their status or resources, remains an ongoing struggle.

In summary, the rule of law stands as a timeless, universal principle, infusing morality into the legal framework. It upholds the ascendancy of law over arbitrary authority, preventing privilege and arbitrariness. By grounding administrative actions in legality, it ensures that government officials and political leaders are accountable to the same laws as every citizen. Upholding due process and judicial oversight, it safeguards justice and equality for all, paving the way for a just and civil society.

---

13. EQUALITY BEFORE the Law: The Pillar of Justice and Democracy

Table of Contents

I. Introduction: The Significance of Equality Before the Law

The second fundamental principle of the rule of law: equality.

The essence of treating all individuals equally under the law.

Ensuring justice and fairness for all, regardless of social or economic status.

II. The Universality of Legal Equality

The principle of equal obedience to common laws of the land.

The absence of special privileges for government officials or the elite.

The jurisdiction of regular courts for all individuals, regardless of status.

III. Compliance with Legislative Laws

The obligation of all individuals to obey laws enacted by legislative bodies.

The role of laws in ensuring order and harmony in society.

The democratic principle of equal submission to laws.

IV. Recognition of Customary Rights and Beliefs

The incorporation of people's rights rooted in customs and traditions.

Protection of religious beliefs and cultural customs.

Upholding diversity and inclusivity within the legal framework.

V. Ensuring Equality in the Legal System

The application of ordinary laws by regular courts.

The principle that the law should apply uniformly to all.

Upholding equality as a foundational aspect of the rule of law.

VI. Accountability of Public Officials

Holding public officials accountable for actions without legal justification.

Shifting away from special protections for government officials.

Chapter 13: Striking a Balance Between Administrative Officer Protection and Accountability

———

Equality Before the Law

I. The Significance of Equality Before the Law

Equality before the law is one of the fundamental pillars of a just and democratic society. It serves as a cornerstone of the rule of law, underlining the importance of impartiality and fairness within the legal system. This principle is not merely an abstract concept but a powerful assertion that justice and democracy hinge upon the equal treatment of every individual under the law.

At its core, equality before the law reaffirms the principle that no one, regardless of their social or economic status, should be exempt from the reach of common laws. This principle is more than a legal doctrine; it is a testament to the bedrock of justice and democracy itself. It ensures that the law is applied uniformly to all citizens, safeguarding their rights and liberties without discrimination.

II. The Universality of Legal Equality

Equality for All: Equality before the law embodies the idea that every individual, irrespective of their social or economic standing, is equally bound by the prevailing laws of the land. It rejects any notion of special privileges or exemptions for government officials or the privileged elite. This principle is the foundation upon which a just society is built, transcending societal divisions and disparities.

Jurisdiction of Regular Courts: A key aspect of this principle is that regular courts hold jurisdiction over all individuals, without regard to their social, economic, or political status. The rule of law insists that justice and legal protection must be accessible to every citizen on an equal footing. It upholds the principle that justice should not be a privilege but a right for all.

III. Compliance with Legislative Laws

Equality before the law encompasses the duty of every individual to abide by the laws established by legislative bodies. These laws are the underpinnings of a harmonious and just society, and they are intended to apply universally. This principle mirrors the democratic ideal that every citizen is equally subject to the laws of the land.

IV. Recognition of Customary Rights and Beliefs

This principle of equality extends to the recognition and respect for people's rights rooted in customs and traditions. It encompasses the protection of religious beliefs and cultural customs, acknowledging the diversity of human societies. By doing so, it ensures that the legal framework respects and accommodates various cultural and religious practices without prejudice.

V. Ensuring Equality in the Legal System

The principle of equality before the law hinges on the consistent and uniform application of ordinary laws by regular courts. It insists that the law should be applied impartially to all individuals, irrespective of their personal characteristics or social standing. Equality is not a peripheral aspect of the legal system but its very essence, ensuring that justice is blind and unbiased.

VI. Accountability of Public Officials

In the pursuit of equality before the law, public officials are held accountable for their actions, particularly when those actions lack legal justification. This represents a significant departure from the era when special protections shielded government officials from legal consequences. Striking a balance between safeguarding administrative officers and ensuring accountability is crucial in upholding the rule of law.

In conclusion, equality before the law serves as a guiding principle that illuminates the path to justice and fairness within any society. It guarantees that every individual, regardless of their social, economic, or political status, is subject to the same legal standards and protections. Upholding this principle is essential for the rule of law to flourish, fostering a just and democratic society where all are treated with the respect and fairness they rightfully deserve.

Chapter 14 - Dominance of the Spirit of the Law: Safeguarding Freedom and Justice

---

I. The Essence of Judicial Decisions in Upholding Rights

The third principle of the rule of law: safeguarding rights.

The role of courts as guarantors of freedom and justice.

The importance of enforcing rights through the legal system.

II. The Role of Judicial Decisions in Protecting Rights

The significance of judicial decisions in interpreting rights.

The judicial role in ensuring that rights are not merely theoretical.

The limitations of written rights without judicial enforcement.

III. The Constitutional System and the Source of Rights

The common law as the source of fundamental freedoms.

The constitutional safeguard of people's rights.

The resilience of rights even during emergencies and crises.

IV. The Judiciary as the Guardian of Individual Rights

The proactive role of the judiciary in securing individual rights.

Amending laws and the constitution to align with justice and equality.

Preventing the misuse of laws and authority for personal gain or power.

V. The Principles of Fairness and Justice

Examining the concept of "bad faith" in administrative decisions.

The implications of "malice" in the exercise of legal powers.

The importance of relevant and rational considerations in decision-making.

VI. Upholding the Rule of Law through Reasonable Decisions

The significance of "unreasonable" decisions in administrative actions.

The judiciary's role in declaring invalid exercises of discretion.

The overarching principle of reasonableness in upholding justice.

VII. Ensuring Checks and Balances in Government

Recognizing the interplay between legislative, executive, and judicial powers.

The importance of legislative and executive branches participating in major disputes.

Preserving the concept of checks and balances for a harmonious government.

VIII. The Rule of Law: A Moral Authority Over Power

The challenge of defining the rule of law.

The supremacy of law as a collective value rather than physical power.

Navigating the delicate balance between government authority and individual freedom.

IX. Administrative Law: A Tool for Governance

The exclusive purpose of administrative law: facilitating administration.

Acknowledging that administrative authorities are not above the law.

The opposition to systems that empower government arbitrariness.

X. Distinguishing Discretion from Arbitrary Power

Differentiating between discretionary and arbitrary powers is crucial.

Arbitrary power poses significant threats to individual freedom and the rule of law.

In the modern world, governments worldwide are increasingly granted authority, necessitating careful scrutiny of how this authority is wielded.

XI. Conclusion: The Ever-Relevant Rule of Law

In conclusion, the dominance of the spirit of the law remains a timeless and ever-relevant principle in modern societies.

It ensures that the law is not just a theoretical concept but a living safeguard of individual rights, justice, and equality.

Upholding the rule of law requires vigilance, a commitment to fairness, and an unwavering dedication to preserving the balance between government authority and individual freedom.

I. The Essence of Judicial Decisions in Upholding Rights

The third pillar of the rule of law, often referred to as the dominance of the spirit of the law, highlights the pivotal role of judicial decisions in safeguarding individual rights. It emphasizes that the law should not remain a theoretical construct but must be actively enforced to protect the liberties and rights of citizens.

II. The Role of Judicial Decisions in Protecting Rights

Central to this principle is the recognition that judicial decisions play a vital role in interpreting and enforcing rights. The judiciary acts as the guardian of these rights, ensuring they are not mere words on paper but tangible protections for individuals. Without the proactive role of the courts, rights may be ignored, limited, or even trampled upon.

III. The Constitutional System and the Source of Rights

In constitutional systems, fundamental freedoms often find their source in common law and are enshrined in written constitutions. These rights are not subject to arbitrary revocation, even during emergencies or declarations of martial law. The judiciary's role is to uphold these rights and ensure they are not infringed upon.

IV. The Judiciary as the Guardian of Individual Rights

The judiciary takes a proactive role in safeguarding individual rights. It can amend laws and even the constitution to align them with principles of justice and equality. The misuse of laws and authority for personal gain or the consolidation of power must be prevented, as it runs counter to the principles of justice and fairness.

V. The Principles of Fairness and Justice

Several legal principles guide the judiciary in upholding the rule of law. "Bad faith" is a term used when discretion is exercised dishonestly or with malicious intent. "Malice" refers to the improper use of legal powers, often involving corruption or dishonesty. "Irrelevant consideration" pertains to decisions that lack rational links between facts and truths.

VI. Upholding the Rule of Law through Reasonable Decisions

"Unreasonable" decisions in administrative actions are deemed arbitrary and are subject to invalidation by the judiciary. Reasonableness stands as an overarching principle in ensuring that justice prevails in all decisions, preventing the misuse of authority.

VII. Ensuring Checks and Balances in Government

The interplay between legislative, executive, and judicial powers is vital for a harmonious government. All branches must participate in major disputes, preserving the concept of checks and balances. This ensures that no single branch becomes overly powerful.

VIII. The Rule of Law: A Moral Authority Over Power

Defining the rule of law can be challenging, as it represents a moral authority over mere physical power. It embodies collective values rather than individual authority. Balancing government authority with individual freedom is crucial, as it upholds justice, equality, and fairness.

IX. Administrative Law: A Tool for Governance

Administrative law serves the exclusive purpose of facilitating government administration. However, it is essential to remember that administrative authorities are not above the law. The opposition to systems that empower government arbitrariness remains a key principle.

X. Distinguishing Discretion from Arbitrary Power

Differentiating between discretionary and arbitrary powers is crucial. Arbitrary power poses significant threats to individual freedom and the rule of law. In the modern world, governments worldwide are increasingly granted authority, necessitating careful scrutiny of how this authority is wielded.

XI. The Ever-Relevant Rule of Law

In conclusion, the dominance of the spirit of the law remains a timeless and ever-relevant principle in modern societies. It ensures that the law is not just a theoretical concept but a living safeguard of individual rights, justice, and equality. Upholding the rule of law requires vigilance, a commitment to fairness, and an unwavering dedication to preserving the balance between government authority and individual freedom.

Chapter 15 - The Exercise of Discretion in Administrative Law: Balancing Power and Accountability

I. The Role of Discretion in Administrative Law

The necessity of administrative discretion.

The absence of separate laws or courts for civil servants.

The significance of resolving conflicts between citizens and the government.

II. The Rule of Law and Its Implications for Administrative Discretion

The requirement for equal submission to the law.

The dangers of special privileges and anarchy.

Inclusion of government agencies within the ambit of the law.

III. Balancing Privileges and Immunities

Multiple individuals holding privileges.

Immunity for judges in the performance of official duties.

The role of laws like The Protection of Officials Act 1893.

Special protections for government officials and foreign diplomats.

Public interest privileges and their impact on government employees.

IV. The Consequence of Judicial Decisions on Individual Rights

The uniqueness of each court case and its impact on private individuals.

The rule of law as a tool to control administrative authority.

The law's supremacy over individual whims and fancies.

The prohibition of harassment except in cases of clear legal violations.

V. Equality Before the Law and Limits on Discretionary Powers

The principle of equality before the law.

Equal protection of the law and its implications for discretionary powers.

The importance of exercising discretion within the boundaries set by law.

VI. Safeguarding Against Abuse of Power by Executives

The need for robust protection against executive abuse of power.

The role of an independent and impartial judiciary.

The importance of fairness, just procedures, and expeditious trials.

I. The Role of Discretion in Administrative Law

Administrative law relies on the prudent exercise of discretion by government officials. Discretion is essential to navigate complex administrative processes, but it must be exercised judiciously to prevent the misuse of power. In some countries, such as France, two distinct court systems exist: administrative courts and ordinary civil courts, each playing a role in resolving conflicts between citizens and the government.

II. The Rule of Law and Its Implications for Administrative Discretion

The rule of law demands equal submission to the law's authority. Any deviation from this principle can lead to anarchy. This principle encompasses government agencies as well, emphasizing that no one is above the law. Even officials, who may have privileges or immunities, must act in accordance with the law and not indulge in arbitrary actions.

III. BALANCING PRIVILEGES and Immunities

In some cases, more than one individual may enjoy privileges. Immunity, especially for judges performing official duties, is a crucial component of many legal systems. Laws like The Protection of Officials Act 1893 provide specific safeguards for officials, and foreign diplomats may also enjoy immunity in court. However, the concept of "public interest privileges" may sometimes shield government employees from injunctions, which raises questions about the equality of justice. Ultimately, the constitution serves as the final authority on these matters.

IV. The Consequence of Judicial Decisions on Individual Rights

Judicial decisions have a profound impact on the rights of private individuals, as each court case involves unique circumstances. Despite potential shortcomings in the definition of the rule of law, it is essential to control and monitor administrative authorities to ensure accountability. The rule of law was conceived for precisely this purpose—to assert the supremacy of law over individual preferences.

V. Equality Before the Law and Limits on Discretionary Powers

The principle of equality before the law dictates that all individuals should receive equal protection of the law. This extends to the exercise of discretionary powers, which must operate within the legal boundaries defined by the law. Such limits help prevent the misuse of discretion and ensure fairness and justice for all.

VI. Safeguarding Against Abuse of Power by Executives

To safeguard against abuse of power by executive authorities, it is imperative to establish robust protections. An independent and impartial judiciary plays a pivotal role in upholding these protections. Furthermore, adherence to fairness, just procedures, and expedient trials is essential to maintain trust in the rule of law.

Striking a Balance in Administrative Discretion

The exercise of discretion in administrative law represents a delicate balance between enabling effective governance and preventing abuse of power. The rule of law, with its emphasis on equality, accountability, and fairness, serves as the cornerstone of this equilibrium. It ensures that no one be it a government official or an ordinary citizen is above the law, and that justice prevails in the exercise of discretionary powers. Maintaining this balance requires vigilance, a commitment to justice, and an unwavering dedication to preserving the rule of law.

Chapter 16: Discretion in the Rule of Law and the Constitution

Balancing Governance and Individual Liberties

I. The Constitution as the Bastion of the Rule of Law

The constitution serves as the unassailable fortress guarding the rule of law within a nation. Within this constitutional framework lies the delicate balance between governance and individual liberties.

1. The Constitutional Framework: The constitution stands as the preeminent legal document, outlining the fundamental principles and norms governing a nation. It delineates the scope of governmental authority, the rights and freedoms of citizens, and the structure within which laws are crafted and executed.

2. Balancing Benefits Programs: The constitution must harmonize benefits programs, designed for societal welfare, with individual freedoms and liberties. Striking this balance is essential to ensure governance promotes the common good while safeguarding individual rights.

3. Emphasizing Fair Play: The rule of law reinforces fair play and emphasizes administrative responsibility. It serves as a guiding light, illuminating the path toward governance that adheres to just and equitable principles.

II. The Role of the Supreme Court in Defining the Rule of Law

The Supreme Court plays a paramount role in shaping the rule of law, acting as the ultimate interpreter of the constitution and providing clarity on the boundaries of executive authority.

1. Pivotal Role: The Supreme Court stands as the vanguard in determining the contours of the rule of law. It delineates the authority delegated to the executive branch, ensuring it operates within carefully defined boundaries.

2. Decisions Based on Known Principles: A cornerstone of the rule of law is that governmental decisions must be based on known principles and rules. Citizens have the right to predictability in governance, understanding when and how government actions may impact them.

III. Preventing Arbitrariness: The Essence of the Rule of Law

The rule of law's core purpose is to prevent arbitrariness in governance, requiring the judicious exercise of discretion within well-defined limits.

1. Understanding Arbitrariness: Arbitrariness poses a fundamental challenge to the rule of law. Balancing discretion is critical to maintaining proper governance while preventing arbitrary actions by the government.

2. The Significance of Guidelines and Norms: To prevent the arbitrary exercise of discretionary powers, it is imperative to establish appropriate guidelines and general norms. These provide a framework within which discretion can operate, offering clarity and consistency.

3. Discretion in the Public Interest: Discretion, when employed, must invariably serve the public interest. It is a tool for advancing the common good, rather than serving individual interests.

IV. Delegated Legislation: A Key Development in Administrative Law

In modern governance, the legislature's constraints necessitate the emergence of delegated legislation, bridging the gap between legislative limitations and the need for effective governance.

1. The Growth of Legislative and Executive Branches: Contemporary times witness a burgeoning legislature and executive branch. However, the legislature alone cannot address the complexities of modern society, necessitating supplementary legislative mechanisms.

2. The Supplementary Nature of Delegated Legislation: Delegated legislation supplements the primary legislative function, enabling administrative authorities to enact specific rules and regulations within the legislative framework.

3. Preventing Misuse through Judicial Oversight: The delegation of legislative authority to administrative bodies entails inherent risks. Judicial oversight acts as a safeguard against misuse, ensuring that delegated legislation aligns with the rule of law and constitutional principles.

V. The Complexity of Modern Legislation and the Role of Administrative Authorities

The increased workload and constraints faced by legislatures necessitate administrative authorities' involvement in bridging the gap between legislatures and citizens.

1. Legislative Constraints: Modern legislatures grapple with constraints stemming from political complexities, time limitations, and the need to address multifaceted national and international issues.

2. The Technical Nature of Subjects: Delegated legislation is crucial for handling technical subjects that demand expert knowledge. Legislators may not possess the specialized understanding required to craft effective laws in these domains.

3. Anticipating Problems: While legislatures decide on specific acts, they can also anticipate potential issues that may arise from their legislation. This forward-thinking approach ensures effective governance and adherence to the rule of law.

In summary, the delicate balance between governance and individual liberties is maintained through the constitutional framework, judicial oversight, and the judicious exercise of discretion within the boundaries set by the rule of law. In an ever-evolving world, preserving this equilibrium remains pivotal for the preservation of democracy and justice.

Chapter 17: Striking the Balance Between Discretion and the Rule of Law

In the intricate tapestry of governance and individual liberties, discretion within the framework of the rule of law and the constitution is a complex interplay that defines the essence of a just and orderly society. At the heart of this interplay lies the constitution itself, serving as the guardian of the rule of law, and thus, the anchor upon which governance operates. This chapter delves into the delicate equilibrium required to maintain the integrity of the rule of law, while also addressing the myriad challenges posed by modern governance, benefits programs, and the exercise of discretionary powers.

I. The Constitution: Bastion of the Rule of Law

The constitution serves as the bedrock upon which the rule of law is built. It is the foundational document that outlines the principles, values, and norms that govern a nation. Within its pages, the constitution delineates the scope of governmental authority, the rights and freedoms of citizens, and the framework within which laws are made and executed. It stands as a testament to the collective will of the people and provides the legal and moral framework for a just society.

Balancing Acts: The constitution's role in striking a balance between benefits programs aimed at societal welfare and individual liberties cannot be overstated. Benefits programs, while crucial for social justice, must coexist harmoniously with the fundamental principles enshrined in the constitution. This balance ensures that governance promotes the common good while safeguarding individual freedoms.

Guiding Principles: The constitution sets forth guiding principles that guide the exercise of discretion by the executive branch and administrative authorities. These principles act as a compass, directing government actions within well-defined boundaries. They serve as a constant reminder that the authority conferred upon the government is not absolute but subject to the rule of law.

II. The Supreme Court's Role in Defining the Rule of Law

The Supreme Court of a country plays a pivotal role in shaping the contours of the rule of law. It serves as the ultimate arbiter in legal matters, interpreting the constitution and providing guidance on the limits of executive authority. Through its decisions, the Supreme Court reinforces the rule of law and ensures that governance remains tethered to well-established legal principles.

Defining Authority: The authority granted to the executive branch, including the exercise of discretionary powers, must operate within the framework established by the Supreme Court. This authority is not boundless; instead, it is carefully circumscribed to prevent overreach and maintain the rule of law.

Known Principles and Predictable Decisions: The Supreme Court emphasizes that decisions made by the government should be based on known principles and rules. Citizens should have a reasonable expectation of the legal principles that will guide government actions. Predictability in governance is essential to ensure that citizens understand when and how government decisions may affect them.

III. Preventing Arbitrariness: The Heart of the Rule of Law

At its core, the rule of law seeks to prevent arbitrariness in governance. Arbitrary actions by the government can erode public trust and undermine the principles of justice and fairness. To maintain the rule of law, discretion must be exercised judiciously, within the limits set by law, and in the public interest.

Balancing Discretion: Balancing discretion within the rule of law is crucial. While the rule of law mandates the prevention of arbitrary actions, it also acknowledges the necessity of discretion for effective governance. Thus, discretion must be wielded judiciously, only to the extent necessary for proper governance.

Guidelines and Norms: To curb the arbitrary use of discretionary powers, appropriate guidelines and general norms must be established. These guidelines act as guardrails, ensuring that discretion is not applied capriciously. They provide a framework within which discretion can be exercised, offering clarity and consistency.

Public Interest as the North Star: Discretion, when applied, must always be in the public interest. The rule of law demands that decisions and actions taken by government authorities prioritize the welfare of the public. In this context, discretion serves as a tool for achieving the common good rather than advancing individual interests.

IV. Delegated Legislation: Bridging Governance Gaps

In the modern landscape of governance, legislative bodies often grapple with constraints that impede their ability to address the complexities of contemporary society comprehensively. Delegated legislation has emerged as a key mechanism for bridging the gap between legislative limitations and the need for effective governance. Administrative authorities, entrusted with technical matters that demand expertise, play a pivotal role in this system.

Supplementary Nature: Delegated legislation is not a substitute for the primary legislative function of a nation's governing body. Instead, it supplements the legislative process by allowing administrative authorities to enact specific rules and regulations within the framework set by parliament or congress.

Expertise and Technical Matters: Delegated legislation is often necessary because the intricate and technical nature of certain subjects requires expert knowledge. Legislators may not possess the specialized understanding required to craft laws that address these complex issues effectively.

Judicial Oversight: The delegation of legislative authority to administrative bodies carries the risk of misuse. To safeguard against such misuse, judicial oversight is essential. Courts play a vital role in ensuring that delegated legislation aligns with the principles of the rule of law and does not overstep its bounds.

V. Striking the Right Balance: Commitment to Fairness, Accountability, and Justice

In navigating the intricate terrain of modern legislation and governance, striking the right balance between discretion and the rule of law is paramount. This balance hinges on a steadfast commitment to fairness, accountability, and justice. It requires the careful calibration of government actions to align with constitutional principles and the common good.

Fairness: Fairness should be the lodestar that guides government actions. Every decision, whether related to benefits programs, administrative responsibilities, or the exercise of discretion, must be rooted in fairness. This ensures that individuals are treated equitably under the law.

Accountability: Government authorities must be held accountable for their actions. Accountability mechanisms, such as judicial oversight and transparency, are essential to prevent abuses of power and maintain the rule of law.

Justice: Ultimately, the rule of law exists to uphold justice. Government actions, when in line with constitutional principles, contribute to a just society. Justice should permeate all aspects of governance, from benefits programs to administrative decisions.

Upholding the Rule of Law

Striking the balance between discretion and the rule of law is an ongoing challenge for constitutional democracies worldwide. It requires unwavering commitment and vigilance to ensure that governance remains just, fair, and accountable. The constitution, with its guiding principles, serves as the North Star, illuminating the path toward a society where the rule of law prevails.

In the complex interplay between governance and individual liberties, the rule of law stands as the cornerstone upon which the edifice of democracy is built. It is a testament to the belief that a just society is one where the principles of fairness, accountability, and justice guide every action of government. As nations continue to navigate the complexities of the modern world, the rule of law remains the steadfast beacon that ensures the rights and liberties of all citizens are protected and upheld.

Did you love *Administrative Law*? Then you should read *Secrets of Mount Kailash, Bermuda Triangle and the Lost City of Atlantis* by Jagdish Krishanlal Arora!

The book goes into the details on the mysteries surrounding Mount Kailash, Bermuda Triangle, and the Lost City of Atlantis. It is also a good book to read for people who like to travel to unknown and mysterious places in the mountains and jungles.

'Secrets of Mount Kailash, Bermuda Triangle, and the Lost City of Atlantis' invites you to explore the world's most intriguing mysteries. Embark on an exhilarating journey as explore the mystique of Mount Kailash's spiritual significance, the enigmatic Bermuda Triangle's tales of disappearances, and the legendary lost city of Atlantis. This book unearths ancient legends, modern investigations, and theories that shroud these place..Join us in uncovering the hidden truths, speculation, and wonder that surround these captivating phenomena."

Also by Jagdish Krishanlal Arora

www.ingramcontent.com/pod-product-compliance
Lightning Source LLC
Chambersburg PA
CBHW072330290526
45794CB00002B/810